Leaders turn Crises into Opportunities

Aditi Chopra

Preface

Quite often we come across people who seem to believe that leaders always succeed and failure for a leader is perceived as a sign of weakness. Frankly, truth couldn't be further from it.

Crises and unexpected events are a natural phenomenon which human beings have no control over and therefore to assume that a leader will never have to deal with a crisis is not natural. Of course, even though we always hope for the best and try our best to avoid failures, a strong leader is one who can fearlessly face a crisis and come out of it as an even stronger leader. I would even say that a seasoned leader can turn a crisis into an opportunity.

We have seen many examples of great leaders and when we read their biographies, we can see how they faced many crises in their career and dealt with them fearlessly. This quality of such people makes them our role models and we learn from their strong leadership. CEO of a company and even the president of a country has to deal with crises. Crises at that level are of much larger magnitude; of course they have a team of advisors and people who can collectively help with the process but the ultimate decision lies with the leader himself.

Dealing with crises is also a skill that leaders need to have in the corporate environment. A strong leader is one who can handle a crisis well and show his leadership in adversity. It is easier to lead when things are going according to plans but a strong leader is the one who can deal effectively under crisis and come out stronger.

So what makes these leaders deal with less than favorable situations and turn them into opportunities? What gives them the courage to move forward? Were they born with these skills or did they acquire these skills along the way?

In this book, I intend to share different aspects of dealing with crises in a corporate environment. I will also talk about skills that leaders need to have or in some cases acquire to deal with unexpected scenarios. I will delve into what works and what doesn't work when dealing with crises.

Aditi Chopra

Leaders turn Crises into Opportunities

CONTENTS

1 CRISIS IN A CORPORATE ENVIRONMENT

When I took my first leadership role in my career, I distinctly remember someone mentioning the term, seasoned leader. To be honest, at that time, I didn't understand it completely. In my mind, I was a confident and able leader but I wondered what did that person mean by "seasoned leader"?

Leaders in every position have to deal with crises in some shape or form. In some cases they turn those crises into opportunities. These leaders deal successfully with every crisis they encounter in their career, and learn from their experiences. They then become seasoned leaders. Seasoned leaders are not afraid of crises anymore because inherently they have the confidence to deal with the unknown. With every successful dealing, their confidence rises.

So what exactly does crisis mean in a corporate environment? Leaders in a corporate environment, no matter which position they are in, are expected to lead people or projects successfully. They are looked upon as pillars of strength and visionaries or a strategist in some cases. They are looked upon as the front-runners who will pave the way for others to follow. In the case of CEOs, basically the whole organization is following their strategy and vision. They forecast the future and build strategies around it. They are always supposed to know which direction to lead towards.

A crisis in very simple terms is the point or moment just prior to a decisive and critical change. An unexpected turn of events that forces leaders to make a critical decision is termed a crisis. **What it forces leaders to do is change or be changed**. Whether they accept it or not, whether they like it or not, they will have to face this critical situation because it is right there in front of them and there is no going back. Leaders who accept a crisis and face it head on are strong leaders. When people don't accept it right away or stay in denial mode, they are forced to make a change and that is never pretty.

It would be ideal to have known about an upcoming crisis and I will talk about that in later chapters but more often than not, a crisis cannot be pre-determined or known in advance. This is the reason it is difficult to handle.

Depending on the scale of the crisis, it could mean several things in a corporate environment. A crisis could occur that may require shuffling of resources. In some cases, a complete change in technology is warranted when it no longer serves the needs of an organization. In other cases a complete re-organization/re-structuring of the organization may take place. A crisis could also mean budget cuts or cancellation of projects. From a people point of view, a corporate crisis could mean that some individuals need to step down from their positions. And in a more severe case, it could mean closing down a division completely or large scale layoffs in the organization.

These crises are unexpected events and can come from any source or direction. They could be financial or technology driven. A lot of times, crises are people driven. Whatever the crisis maybe, leaders have to face it and take the best decision they can make at a given point in time, from the information that they have. Even if leaders wished they knew more about the situation, they have to go with what they know at that point in time. As long as the leaders take into account all the information they have and make the best possible decision, they have nothing to regret later. Hindsight is always 20/20 but you can't have all the information to base the decision, in the time of a crisis. The more important thing is to make a good decision.

Let's look at some examples of crises in a corporate environment.

Example 1: If a manager relies heavily on an employee to accomplish his goals in the organization and that employee suddenly decides to leave the company or transfer to a different organization for one reason or another, it is a moment of crisis. It is something that the leader has to deal with. It would have been nice if he had done succession planning for the employee but if he didn't, it certainly is a difficult spot to be in.

Example 2: If an engineer fixes a software problem and releases the software to the customer and pretty soon realizes that he has in fact introduced two more new problems, it is a moment of crisis for the engineer. Had he done a thorough analysis of his fix in an environment similar to the customer, he could have possibly avoided the problem. But perhaps, he didn't have access to the customer environment for testing and he did the best he could. But now, he has to deal with the crisis.

Example 3: If company finances are in trouble, it is a critical moment and the leadership team may decide to restructure the employee pay structure in order to deal with the crisis. If the compensation change is negative, it is a very sensitive change and needs to be handled with a lot of care. This kind of crisis has multiple repercussions and is certainly not an easy one to deal with.

Example 4: When a product fails to perform its function in a customer environment and causes the customer some financial loss, a crisis occurs. This can cause severe repercussions in several departments of the company. The outcome could be anywhere from losing the customer and their loyalty to brand quality issue for the company and losing business with other customers. Marketing, Customer Account team and engineering leaders have to deal with such crises.

The few scenarios above illustrate the point that every leader, irrespective of their position needs to deal with a crisis in a corporate environment. The nature and scale of the crisis may be different at every level, but leaders need to be able to deal with these uncertain situations.

2 SOURCE OF A CRISIS

No leader wants to deal with a crisis but it can happen anytime and can come from any direction or source. When a leader assumes a certain role, he needs to be prepared to handle critical situations. No matter how much leaders prepare to avoid a crisis, they must have the skills to deal with one when they come across it.

At a high level, we can categorize sources of crises into two types. Most of the time crises are triggered from external sources but sometimes the sources can be internal as well.

External Crises

These crises are coming from sources outside of the individual leader.

- **People Crisis**

    It can be a crisis for a leader when people around him do not support his initiative, thought, vision or strategy. In the corporate environment, leaders depend a lot on others to carry out their vision or strategy. Lack of support from people in the organization can be a huge crisis to overcome. This can be even more critical if you are new to the organization that you leading in.

- **Technology Crisis**

If an organization has been relying on a certain technology to perform its functions but for some reason, it fails to fulfill the organizations' goals and objectives, it is also a moment of crisis that a leader has to deal with. Sometimes it could be scale issue or functional issue which hinders a particular technology to not serve the purpose anymore. The big decision is which other technology to replace with? Various considerations could be - What additional functionality is needed to solve the crisis?; Can enhancements be added or a total replacement is needed? Cost/timeline/training etc. needs to be considered as factors to make the decision. The leader also has to decide, at the same time, how to continue in the interim while the new technology is being prepared to be introduced.

- **Customer Related Crisis**

If the customer's environment is negatively affected by a company's product or customer satisfaction is compromised in any other way, this could mean a crisis for multiple leaders in a company. For most companies, customer comes first and it is the right strategy to adopt. Dealing with a customer related crisis requires a lot of patience and skills. This crisis doesn't only affect the leader but also the reputation of the company.

- **Organization level Crisis**

While we cannot minimize crisis for a leader at any level, we cannot deny the fact that a crisis is the hardest to deal with for highest ranking officials. Along with dealing with the crisis itself, the visibility is really high for someone like a CEO.

CEOs and other high-ranking leaders often have to lead corporation wide changes when they face a crisis. These crises could be financial or a complete strategy change due to competition in the market or some other external factor. Employees of the corporation going through these changes are sometimes not satisfied with the way these crises are handled, but they also have to deal with them in their own way. Any unknown scenario that warrants an organization level change is a large scale crisis such as layoffs or pay reduction or re-organization. These crises are never easy to deal with and affects the whole organization.

Internal Crises

Sometimes a crisis can be internal to the leader.

• Family Crisis

A leader may have to deal with family crisis because of which he is not able to continue with his role for a certain amount of time. Although family crisis affects only that particular individual, it also has its repercussions on the career aspect and the leader in this case has to lean on his colleagues for support. In this case, it depends on how strong of a support network the leader has, to get through the crisis.

• **Personal Leadership Crisis**

If the leader facing the unknown situation is not skilled or ready to take on such a scenario, then it is an internal crisis for him. It is possible that he took on a role that he was not ready for and is unable to handle the situation. He is stuck with the situation and doesn't know how to approach it. He may have been over-confident about his skills when he signed up for this role. I like to think of confidence as - Not knowing 100% about a job role but believing that one can handle whatever is unknown. One can never know everything about a situation or job position but having that confidence to handle the unknown is very important before one signs up for a position.

I have illustrated different sources of crises above. While this list is not exhaustive, you get the idea that each crisis has its own parameters and has to be handled in a different manner. The skills required to deal with each could also be different. One thing a leader under crisis needs to have is inner confidence to be able to deal with the unknown.

3 USING INTUITION

Wouldn't it be nice if we had a detector for a crisis that could give us warning in advance? If so, every leader would want to have that detector and that would certainly give him a lot of confidence. But of course there is no such detector. What some of the leaders do have is the power of intuition.

Intuition is a trait that helps leaders in unprecedented scenarios. When situations and scenarios are obvious and straightforward, intuition doesn't help much but it is a very powerful tool during uncertain scenarios. Some people refer to intuition as a gut feeling.

I would encourage every leader to go through the MBTI assessment for self-awareness. MBTI (Myers-Briggs Type Indicator) assessment can tell you if you are intuitive or how intuitive you are. Not everybody is born with an intuitive mindset. If your MBTI assessment tells you that you are not intuitive, you can perhaps partner with an intuitive person and brainstorm with him in situations where you are stuck or need help. These people are able to listen to various signs and signals and detect that something is wrong.

On the other hand, if you are an intuitive person, you should certainly take advantage of this skill. Learn to rely on your intuition. Learn to base decisions upon it. And don't ignore your intuitive signals. You will find that it works.

Leadership involves learning and practicing various soft skills, it is not as straightforward as exercising technical skills. Leaders often run into situations where it is not obvious which path to take or which decision to make. Even though you run through the pros and cons and risks involved, ultimately what guides you is your intuition.

Intuition combined with experience is a very powerful combination. However, highly intuitive leaders should remember that they are not 100% right all the time. Therefore, they need to be mindful when they are basing decisions on intuition. If you are highly intuitive, perhaps you should work with a non-intuitive person and check your hunches against his opinions.

Let me explain this concept with a few examples.

Example 1: I recall in my engineering days, my company was experimenting with a new Operating System software for our products. We had a solid base of products that ran on our existing Operating System (OS). This existing OS technology however, had its limitations and some engineers wanted to overcome these limitations by moving to a new technology. There was a lot of buzz in the company about this new OS and I was also given the opportunity to work on it for my product line. To be honest, I felt honored in the beginning to work on this latest and greatest technology. As I began to work on it, I realized that the new technology had its own drawbacks. I also sensed from talking to fellow engineers that there was an underlying issue but the buzz for the new OS was still going strong in the company. I asked my manager to move me back to the group that worked on the older technology and I cited my own reason for the move. I later realized that my intuition was correct because six months later the new OS project was scrapped. I relied on my intuition and therefore prevented a crisis from happening. The engineers who were working on the new OS were asked to find other jobs within the company and that was a moment of crisis for them.

Example 2: In another scenario, I was once asked to take on a project that no one wanted to work on. At first, I hesitated a little bit but after talking to a couple of people I learned that this project was important from a customer satisfaction perspective. I knew that our company paid a lot of attention to customer satisfaction and it was part of the overall company strategy. I relied on my intuition and took on the project even though I knew that no one else wanted it. Three months into the project, after doing my own analysis of it, I found a few potholes which when covered would make this project really useful for the organization. I charted my proposal and circulated it with the leadership team and got a go ahead. A year later, this project became the most coveted project in our organization. Everyone wanted to be associated with this project.

I can cite many more such examples, but the key point here is – if you are intuitive, trust your signals and learn to use them to your advantage. If however, you are not intuitive yourself, team up with someone who is and learn from their perspective. This skill can help you in early detection of a crisis in some shape or form.

4 LEADERSHIP DURING A CRISIS

We have discussed the importance of successfully dealing with a crisis. So what makes a leader deal successfully with a crisis? How do leaders turn these crises into opportunities?

I talked about seasoned leader in Chapter One. These leaders draw upon their previous experiences when dealing with a complicated situation. But let's just say when an un-seasoned leader has to face a crisis, how does he deal with it? Is he born with the skills or does he acquire them along the way? Is there a common trait of these leaders irrespective of their leadership style which makes them deal with the crisis?

Finding your inner strength

I tend to believe that each individual has three sides to them. One side is that part of yourself that only you know. The second side is what others see, but that you may be unaware of its existence or let's just say how others perceive you. And then there is that side that no one knows – not yourself or others.

The side of you that no one knows holds the potential that you or anyone else has yet to discover about yourself. It is where a hidden strength lies within you which has not yet been explored. When faced with a crisis, leaders draw upon this hidden strength to face up to the situation.

By drawing upon the hidden strength, leaders explore infinite possibilities for success. The usual methods of dealing will not work in a crisis situation. To assume that you will fly by without making any change or without drawing upon your hidden strength, is wrong. Sometimes we are used to doing things in a certain way because that's how we have always done it until we face a crisis and we realize we have to change our thinking. The sooner you realize that, the better equipped you are to deal with the unknown situation.

Your previous experiences may have been great but if those experiences do not help with the present, don't hold on to them. Welcome change, when it is required. As they say – **"Change is the only constant in life"**. Leaders should look upon these moments of crises as an opportunity to grow as a leader. One can only grow when one faces the situation head on and makes the right decision. An open mind works best in these cases. When one is open to changing the way one has always worked, it opens various paths for success.

Think about it, if the situation is new, then wouldn't a new kind of response be warranted?

Let's take a look at how a leader should approach various crises:

- **People Crisis**

When faced with a people crisis i.e. not getting enough support from individuals in the organization, a leader needs to look within. He will need to evaluate why he is not getting support from others. Is it because his strategy is flawed or is it his personality that is not appealing to people? Or it could be that whatever he is proposing is not going to add value? And if he firmly believes that his strategy will add value, is it that he has not been able to articulate his vision enough for people to understand? He needs to do an honest evaluation of what can he change about his strategy and/or communication aspect that can help people see his vision. By finding the right answer this leader turns a crisis into an opportunity for growth in his skills.

- **Technology Crisis**

If a technology is not serving the purpose of an organization anymore, then an evaluation is warranted. The leader needs to decide if a replacement is needed or enhancement of existing technology will suffice. Since there will be costs associated with the replacement especially if it is a companywide usage, enough diligence needs to be done to choose a replacement such that it is an appropriate change. You don't want to run into a scenario where the replacement is worse than the prior technology. That would mean one step forward and two steps backwards. Relying on the right set of advisors and doing a thorough research will help mitigate the risk. This leader can also look upon this change as an opportunity for fulfilling other goals with new technology that this organization was not able to fulfill with previous technology.

- **Customer Related Crisis**

CRM (Customer Relationship Management) is a model for managing a company's interactions with current and future customers. It is very important to manage a customer related crisis adequately, both for the functional aspect of it but also for maintaining future relationship with the customer. Failing to do so will result in losing the customer as well as impacting the relationship with other customers when the word gets around. When a customer related crisis happens, typically an organization makes an internal change to reflect what has happened and to prevent such a crisis from happening again. Communicating to the customer about what measures are being taken within the organization goes a long ways towards building a strong customer relationship. If this leader makes the appropriate change in the organization, he has not only dealt with the crisis but also turned it into an opportunity of growth for the organization itself.

- **Organization level Crisis**

A large scale crisis such as layoffs or pay reduction or re-organization is never easy to deal with and affects the whole organization.

Transparency and clear communication are very much a necessity in these cases. When Leaders are completely transparent about the reason for the change, they earn trust and respect of the organization. Failing to do so will have its own repercussions and may spur more crises such as employee turnover, morale issues etc. Leaders should look upon these crises as an opportunity to build a stronger trust with their employees.

- **Family Crisis**

When dealing with family or personal health issues, a leader needs to acknowledge the fact that his emotional state is not healthy enough to take on serious issues at work. Recognizing that and asking for help is not a sign of weakness. On the contrary, it is the wise thing to do both for the leader and the corporation he works for. His energy has to be focused on dealing with family issues and once they are resolved, he can focus back again on his work.

- **Personal Leadership Crisis**

This is a tricky scenario to deal with. In this case, there is no external factor involved, the crisis is internal to the leader himself. He has probably taken on more than he can chew. So what should he do in such a scenario? Should he ignore the internal turmoil or face it?

My advice would be to face it head-on, recognize it early on and make a decision rather than have it linger on and assume that it is going to go away on its own. In such cases, the issue doesn't go away, instead it keeps getting worse. Taking an action earlier rather than later is better for everyone involved. If a leader has taken on more than he can handle, it is okay to admit that to himself and others and bow out of what he cannot handle. If un-addressed, this internal crisis can become more serious and can cause more issues down the road. This leader needs to look upon this as an opportunity for internal growth and do a self-analysis on what kind of job positions are more suited to his leadership style and skills. In some cases, he may decide to acquire a new skill or look for a position more suited to his strengths.

We have looked at various critical situations and how leaders deal with them depending on the crisis at hand. No matter what the nature of the crisis was or what style the leaders adopted, each of these leaders have one thing in common. They draw upon their internal strength to make the right decision to deal with the situation. They face the situation head-on, take the right decision and turn a crisis into an opportunity for growth.

5 COMMUNICATION DURING A CRISIS

While there are many aspects of dealing with a crisis, communication demands special mention here. We cannot emphasize enough the importance of communication in the corporate environment. No matter what kind of crisis a leader is facing, he has to be able to communicate with the relevant stakeholders about different aspects of the situation and how they will be affected by it. This is crucial to the situation. Once the leader has understood the impact and come to a conclusion or decision, he must communicate to the right audience. This will build trust and necessary environment for everyone to deal with the situation.

How you communicate, when you communicate and who do you communicate with makes all the difference. This becomes even more crucial in the case of a crisis. A leader must identify all stakeholders that need to be notified about the crisis at hand and how he plans to handle it. The more you communicate with the stakeholders, the better equipped you will be to handle the situation and get a more favorable response. The natural tendency in the case of a crisis might be to not communicate until the situation has been completely controlled. But there might be few stakeholders who will need to be involved right from the beginning to ensure that the right decisions are being taken. These few stakeholders might help in making the right decision from the start.

Following are some useful communication tips :

- **Manage Expectations**: A main component of communication is managing expectations. Effective communication helps in managing all the stakeholders' expectations. You ought to set goals upfront and communicate them in order to avoid any misunderstanding during the moment of crisis.

- **Targeted Communication**: Targeted communication is a must for effectiveness. In the moment of crisis, don't communicate everything to everyone, tailor it for the audience. Sensitive information does not need to be communicated to everyone as it may cause panic. Get the right audience involved from the start and later communicate the decision made to others.

- **Get Feedback**: When handling critical situations, don't just communicate your strategy to deal with the situation, ask for feedback as well. This is where collective leadership can help mitigate the risks. The leaders that you consult with can bring in their experience to the mix and help out in the decision making.

- **Don't Be Afraid**: Don't be afraid to be the whistle blower, sometimes it is needed. People may be shy to call out a bad situation out of fear of repercussions, but sometimes it is a necessary evil.

Let me cite an example here to explain what I mean by the importance of communication.

In one of my projects, my team was responsible for corporate wide data. There were multiple dashboard teams involved that were feeding off of the data provided by my team which increased the visibility of my team and project. When we were at year end of our cycle, my team realized that there was an inherent limitation in the database which will not allow our data feed to reach all the dashboard teams in time to make the yearly switch. The dashboards had companywide visibility and it was very important for them to show the correct data on a daily basis.

It was a crisis I needed to deal with and I didn't know which solution would be the right one for most teams. I had my ideas on how to proceed but what I decided to do was call a meeting right away with all stakeholders (one representative from each of the dashboard teams). At that meeting, I explained to them the issue that my team was facing and how it would affect them. It was not an easy thing to do but was necessary such that everyone understood the impact.

We then collectively decided to delay the data feed to these dashboard teams until the database issue was worked within my team. The fix would take up to three months. We also came up with a temporary solution that would accommodate these dashboards to show the correct data in the interim.

Although it was not so good news that I had communicated, I was actually praised by my supervisors to communicate it well in time and keeping all stakeholders abreast of the situation. I prevented another crisis from happening by communicating to the right audience at the right time.

6 THE EMOTIONAL ELEMENT

Whether we acknowledge it or not, there is certainly a human and/or emotional element associated with a leader facing a crisis. He is very much aware of his visibility in the organization and how he is going to be perceived and/or be judged by his decisions during tough times.

It is the natural tendency of human beings to feel a certain amount of pressure from peers or supervisor when dealing with a crisis. The higher the position, the greater the pressure and visibility.

Sometimes the visibility and pressure can paralyze people from taking action. They could be so afraid of taking the wrong decision that they will not take any decision at all. It is the fear of public failure. It is the fear of being judged.

All I can say is, leaders should not be afraid to fail in public. Everyone has made some mistakes at a certain point or another so who is anyone to judge? Most of the times, people who are judging might even perform worse than the leader in question. Unless they have walked in the same shoes, they have no authority to judge anyone else.

Of course a leader in crisis should do due diligence before taking a decision but he should not be afraid to take action. He should not be afraid to fail or be judged by others. If one is not sure of their decision, they can always consult a few trusted colleagues before taking action but they shouldn't shy away from it. It is therefore very important to have a network of trusted confidantes around you and have that network of people to lean on in times of distress.

If one is afraid of what others will think and how they will judge, then one is not ready for a leadership role and certainly not a critical leadership role.

7 LEADERSHIP AFTER A CRISIS

A good leader is one who is constantly sharpening his leadership skills. I would be surprised if anyone believed that they have learned everything there is to learn about leadership. Leadership concepts are evolving every day and even if one has learned all the skills, one can still polish them.

If a leader wants to do self-analysis after having dealt with a crisis, a powerful tool to apply is SWOT (Strengths Weaknesses Opportunities and Threats) analysis. In the marketing world, we do a SWOT analysis for a product to identify where it would fit in the bigger picture and how to position it in its target market. This tool can be also used for self-analysis to determine how one can sharpen one's leadership skills.

SWOT Analysis

SWOT analysis is a structured planning tool that is used to evaluate the Strengths, Weaknesses, Opportunities, and Threats. A SWOT analysis can be done for a product, place, industry or person. It involves specifying the objective of the business venture or project and identifying the internal and external factors that are favorable and unfavorable to achieving that objective. When performed for a person, the objective would be to improve leadership skills such that a leader can become more seasoned.

Strengths: Skills that a leader possesses that give him an advantage over others.
Weaknesses: These are characteristics that a leader has a disadvantage relative to others.
Opportunities: Where does a leader see scope for exploration that he hasn't taken advantage of.
Threats: These are elements in the corporate environment that could cause trouble for the leader in the future.

Identification of SWOTs is important because they help the leader identify areas that are potential threats in future and also scope for improvement that would minimize the threats.

Although typically a SWOT analysis is done by the leader himself, it would also benefit if he could get a couple of trusted colleagues to give him input on the four areas. Sometimes we ourselves may be blinded to a certain weakness or may not see all the threats ourselves. Getting a honest input in all four areas will make the SWOT analysis exercise more fruitful.

SWOT diagrams are generally drawn in a quadrant format with Strengths and Weaknesses as the top two quadrants and Opportunities and Threats as the bottom two quadrants. Having them side to side gives a clear picture for evaluation. By looking at possible threats, one can get a better picture of which possible weakness to overcome or which strength to hone in on more.

Let's take a look at some examples of how doing a SWOT analysis can help leaders polish their leadership skills.

Example 1:

A leader in one of the organizations I worked in combined her 360 degree feedback with her SWOT analysis. A 360 degree feedback is feedback that comes from members of a leader's immediate work circle. Most often, 360-degree feedback will include direct feedback from an employee's subordinates, peers, and supervisor(s), as well as a self-evaluation. When she looked at her strengths, she realized that she was almost always praised by her superiors for her abilities to lead. Her 360 degree feedback comments highlighted one of her threats from her own team. One of her team members expressed dissatisfaction on his interaction with her as a manager. When she looked at her weaknesses, she realized that it matched up with her threats because she dealt with her superiors about 90% of her time and she didn't have a lot of time to spend with her own team members.

The SWOT analysis made her aware of her weakness and she decided to make more time in her schedule to meet with her own team members on a one-on-one basis. This change made her more aware of her team members' issues and challenges. By making this change, she mitigated the risk of potential threats from her own team members.

Example 2:

In another SWOT analysis done by one of my peers, this leader looked at his strengths. He was constantly being praised by his supervisors for excellent leadership qualities and great potential. They didn't point out as such any weakness for him to improve upon but he found that they all saw great potential in him. His SWOT chart didn't point at any particular weakness to work on or worry about any particular threats. However, some of his superiors did point out some training avenues as an opportunity for growth. Since he was a natural leader, he was good at what he did but he could certainly use these training sessions to hone in on his leadership qualities. These training sessions would allow him to explore his true potential and he decided to allocate a certain amount of time in his schedule to sign up for appropriate training.

I would recommend leaders to explore the SWOT analysis tool to hone in on their leadership qualities.

Aditi Chopra

8 LEARNING FROM A CRISIS

It is very important to learn from a crisis after the storm has passed. This kind of learning can be valuable and can be passed down to others for learning purposes.

Let's look at how we can learn from a crisis and what we can do in order to effectively use the learning.

Post Crisis Analysis

Most organizations require that a Post Project Assessment be done after completion of a project. Similarly a post analysis of a crisis will help. We can do a root cause analysis to figure out if we could have prevented a crisis or how can we prevent such crises in future? The leader who has faced the crisis can call this meeting to discuss and perform a post crisis analysis or have someone else facilitate it.

Conducting such an analysis is not a finger pointing exercise unlike the perception people have. Most people shy away from doing a post crisis analysis due to this perception. In reality what they are losing is the ability to learn from the experience and utilize it for the future.

The key to conducting a good post crisis analysis is to keep things impersonal. This is not the time to criticize someone's leadership style. This is the time to learn from the experience, what was done successfully and what could have been dealt with differently. This is not a leadership feedback session, it is a crisis assessment session.

When we learn from these sessions and apply the learning to the organization or project, it can have a long term impact. I have been in such sessions where we brought all our findings to the table for senior leaders to assess and discuss.

In some post analysis sessions, what came out of such meetings is a rehash of RACI (Responsible, Accountable, Consulted, Informed) matrix. When multiple parties are involved in a certain project or program, sometimes lines of responsibilities can be fuzzy and things can fall through the cracks. By doing a post assessment of a situation, one can re-assess if the responsibilities need to re-assigned. It also puts everyone on the same page and brings transparency in communication. This is even more important if the teams are virtual where communication plays a very important role.

In another post crisis analysis session, we decided to institute changes in our program. New initiatives were spawned that placed the right hooks in the program to prevent a similar crisis from happening again.

Learning from a crisis is an absolute must in my opinion. There are so many takeaways from these situations for everyone.

RACI model

The RACI model is a straightforward tool that can be used for identifying roles and responsibilities among different people in an organization. This is especially useful when the programs are large and involve cross-functional interactions. RACI provides a clear picture of what needs to be done and by whom. It is usually depicted by a chart and can be easily performed in Microsoft excel format. The idea is to identify who is Responsible for a task, who is Accountable, who needs to be kept Informed and who should be Consulted for different aspects of the task. RACI may be an overhead for smaller teams but I would strongly recommend it for larger teams.

The following steps are performed in a RACI session:

- Identify all the activities or tasks to be performed and list them down on the left hand side of the chart.

- Identify all the roles in the organization and list them at the top of the chart.

- Complete the chart by identifying who is Responsible, Accountable, Consulted and Informed for each of the activities or tasks.

- Every task should have one person Responsible. When there is no "R" for a process, that is a gap which will need to be addressed.

- Address gaps and/or overlaps. Overlaps are generally not a good idea as it can muddy the responsibilities.

Spawn Initiatives

Following a post crisis analysis, if the takeaway is to introduce a change in the organization or customer interaction change is warranted, the right thing to do is to spawn such initiatives. This was the whole point of doing a post analysis so we can make the much needed change. It is not essential that there is always an initiative that is required, sometimes the learning is more personal or a communication gap is identified. But occasionally a large scale initiative may be required to make a systemic change in the organization.

For example, when I inherited a software team, I realized that we were getting a huge number of customer problems and my team was sometimes working on weekends to solve these critical customer problems. I didn't have a lot of history of the software since I inherited it. What I decided to do is call a post analysis meeting to discuss all the customer problems. After doing a thorough analysis, we spun a couple of initiatives within the larger team to address quality issues related to our test environment. Our test environment did not emulate customer network and hence we were never able to catch the problems. These problems became critical when uncovered at the customer's premises because they needed to be addressed under pressure.

9 WHY PEOPLE FAIL TO DEAL WITH A CRISIS

Sometimes leaders are not able to deal with a crisis successfully in spite of their good intentions and efforts. While this is not the ideal scenario, it is a possibility for sure.

There could be several reasons why; let's look at some of these reasons in detail.

- **Being paralyzed by fear of failure** - I talked about this in Chapter Six. Fear of being judged by peers or fear of taking the wrong decision can sometimes paralyze the leader from taking any action whatsoever. They may go into a loop of thinking what-if scenarios or the worst case scenarios and never decide which path to take. This kind of thinking is sometimes termed as 'analysis paralysis'. It would be wise to team up with another individual who can nudge this leader into taking action.

- **Not being able to draw on their inner strength** - Perhaps this leader is not ready to take that important step to draw on his inner strength and decide how to deal with a crisis. While drawing on inner strength may be easier to do for certain leaders, it could be very difficult for others. There are a lot of scenarios that are not pretty when leaders come across crises and they are not able to draw upon this strength. In these cases, they will not be able to perform.

- **Not having a strong support system to rely on** – If a leader has not spent time building a trusted network of people around him, he may not have enough support system in the time of need. He may only realize the absence of such a system when he faces his first crisis. It probably did not even occur to him before that he needed such a network.

- **Too large to handle** - If a leader deals with a crisis of such a large magnitude that he is not ready to face given his experience, he will not be able to deal with it. He probably signed up for a role larger than his capability at a certain point of time.

What is important in these cases is for the leader to be able to recognize these situations as an opportunity for personal growth. It is not as important for him to succeed as to be able to learn from these experiences and take the right action to prepare for future. If he takes the right action going forward and is able to deal with a similar situation, then he has already accomplished quite a bit. He has achieved personal growth!

10 HOW TO PREPARE IN ADVANCE

It is never too late to acquire the right skills or to prepare in advance for critical situations. Every leader will have to deal with a crisis in some shape or form in his career and therefore it is very important to prepare in advance.

In order for leaders to prepare in advance for dealing with unknown situations, there are multiple measures they can adopt.

Develop Intuitive Skills

I am a highly intuitive person and I didn't go through any training to acquire my intuitive skills. I have heard of such programs that train people to acquire some intuitive skills to help recognize signs. As I discussed in Chapter Three, intuition helps a great deal in getting some early signals and therefore it is worth exploring such skills if one doesn't naturally possess them.

The first step is to take a MBTI assessment to gain more self-awareness. If you don't possess such intuitive skills, team up with someone who is intuitive so you can bounce off ideas with them.

Another way to develop intuitive skills is to look back on an event in your life. Try to analyze and see if there were any signs before the crisis that you possible ignored? Were there any minor events that you ignored thinking this is going to go away or is not important enough? Could you have possibly stringed together some of these minor events to detect a possible crisis?

Networking

While I was studying for my MBA degree, one concept was emphasized quite a bit. We were encouraged to attend various networking events and I realized that in the business world, it is a must skill to have. I would encourage everyone in the business world to embrace networking. It helps you build relationships. When you build strong relationships, you learn from them and they can help you in the time of need. However don't just go through the motions. Here are a few tips on effective networking.

• **Make it second habit**: Make networking a way of life. You shouldn't have to think "I am going to do networking now." You should unconsciously network whether you are at a social, work or family event. It will be hard in the beginning but once you get the hang of it, it will seem quite natural. I say this from experience. I used to be very shy at networking events when I worked as an engineer but I trained myself and pretty soon, I didn't even have to think about it. If you don't want to go at it alone, tag a friend or associate along who is good at it and learn from them.

• **Don't always look for bottom-line**: Don't

attend a networking event only when you think you will get something out of it. Often people wonder what is in it for me and how will I benefit from it? And if they don't find anything interesting, they bail out. Remember that sometimes when you attend an event, you give back and it is very fulfilling. Other times, you learn by simple observation. You make contacts that are not obviously useful in the beginning but they will be at a later point in time.

• **Relate to people**: When you meet people at networking events, make a genuine effort to relate to them. Go beyond the usual exchange of work titles. Ask them about their aspirations and/or personal life. See how you can help them in their mission. Make an effort to understand their goals and think how you can align your goals with theirs. Give them something to remember you for. Try and help them before you expect help from them.

• **Follow through**: Keep in touch with people after you meet them at networking events through email, social media, phone, etc. Look for commonality with them; this will help you to keep in touch.

Observation

There are basically three avenues that a leader learns from – education, experience and emulation. If a leader is not seasoned yet, he can observe other leaders in the industry and simply learn by understanding how these seasoned leaders deal with crises.

You will be surprised by how much you can learn by observation. You can take notes or even ask these seasoned leaders to mentor you in the skills that you want to acquire from them. Sometimes by simple observation, you may not come to know of some of the crisis they are dealing with but if ask to be mentored, you may learn more in details from their experiences. Emulating these strong leaders is a good way of learning from their experiences. This prepares you for the unknown and also gives you some self-confidence.

Succession Planning

If a leader heavily depends on a talented and strong employee, it pays to do some succession planning for this employee in case he decides to leave or has to take a long term leave for any purpose. You cannot do succession planning for all positions, it is just not feasible but I would recommend it for some key positions. I have seen very few instances where leaders actively conduct succession planning but in some cases, it is required. Similarly for critical resources, we need to have backup such that we don't a single point of failure.

Conduct Audits

In a large organization, sometimes the processes may not be completely understood by each and every group that is supposed to follow it. Even if people are trained, sometimes changes happen in processes which may not get communicated across the board. Conducting audits periodically can ensure that each process is being followed the way it was supposed to. Such audits can help prevent crisis by ensuring proper usage of process and technology.

ABOUT THE AUTHOR

Aditi Chopra is a seasoned leader in the software industry. She has a passion for helping people succeed in their careers and is motivated to share her knowledge through her books. She has authored two popular books on leadership skills titled "Ten Mistakes A Manager Should Avoid" and "Leading Without Authority".